D0426771

P7

TEENAGE DRINKING

TEENAGE DRINKING

Elaine Landau

—Issues in Focus—

ENSLOW PUBLISHERS, INC.

44 Fadem Road
Box 699
Springfield, N.J. 07081
U.S.A.

P.O. Box 38
Aldershot
Hants GU12 6BP
U.K.

Copyright © 1994 by Elaine Landau

All rights reserved.

No part of this book may be reproduced by any means
without the written permission of the publisher.

Library of Congress Cataloging-in-Publication Data

Landau, Elaine.
    Teenage drinking / by Elaine Landau.
        p. cm. — (Issues in focus)
    Includes bibliographical references and index.
    ISBN 0-89490-575-9
    1. Teenagers—United States—Alcohol use—Juvenile literature.
    2. Alcoholism—Prevention—Juvenile literature.   [1. Alcoholism. 2. Alcohol.]
    I. Title. II. Series: Issues in focus (Hillside, N.J.)
    HV5066.L425 1994
    362.29'2'0835—dc20   94-40
                                              CIP
                                              AC

Printed in the United States of America

10 9 8 7 6 5

Illustration Credits: Arizona S.A.D.D., p. 32; The Century Council, p. 58; Clear
Brook Lodge, p. 75; Linda B. Ledger, pp. 13, 35, 46, 48; Courtesy of New Jersey
Department of Health, Department of Law & Public Safety, Division of State
Police, p. 28; Sparta *Independent*, p. 26, 39; The South Dakota Division of Alcohol
& Drug Abuse, 68; State of Alaska, Department of Health & Social Services,
Division of Alcohol & Drug Abuse, p. 80; State of New Jersey, Department of Law
& Public Safety, Division of State Police, p. 24; Students Against Driving Drunk,
"Contract For Life" pp. 83.

Cover Illustration: J. Greenberg, Unicorn Stock Photos

Contents

Foreword 6

1 Alcohol—A Destructive Drug 7

2 Drinking and Driving 21

3 Young Drinkers 37

4 Seeing the Signs 55

5 The Family Response 62

6 Getting Help 73

Students Against Driving Drunk
(S.A.D.D.) "Contract For Life" 83

Resource Directory 85

Notes by Chapter 97

Further Reading 99

Index 101

About the Author 104

Foreword

While writing this book, I spoke to many teens trying to contend with the often overwhelming effects of alcohol abuse. The young people were in various stages of this dilemma, and many of their experiences were both personal and extremely painful. Often their stories were sadly similar and, in the majority of cases, publication of these interviews was contingent on my disguising their identities. Therefore, the profiles within this text are composites—they are the sagas of one and many at the same time. Frequently they represent the conflicts of a generation in flux.

1

Alcohol—A Destructive Drug

Shannon (age 13)

"I idolized my father when I was small. I thought of him as a storybook prince and couldn't wait till he came home each night so he could sweep me up in his arms and tell me I was his pretty princess.

"I don't know exactly when things began to change. Maybe that's because it happened gradually. But after a while my father stopped delighting in me. He didn't even look glad to see me anymore. As soon as he came through the door, he'd just say, 'Boy, I need a drink after the day I've had.'

"But his first drink was never his last and before long I began to think that my father only had bad days since he always acted that way. The days of him lifting me up to touch the ceiling or whirling me around the room were gone. I was bigger now and my father was quick to remind me that I'd become too heavy for our living-room athletics. After I'd put on some weight, he stopped calling me princess. Instead he nicknamed me 'piglet.'

"I used to miss the time I spent with my father, but then I decided that I didn't really need him. I guess my mother felt the same way because she threw him out of the house that summer while I was away at camp. Nobody told me about it until camp was over, because they hadn't wanted to ruin my vacation. But when I saw my mother standing all alone next to our station wagon to take me home, I knew that something was up and that it was bad.

"From then on it was my mother who began drinking heavily and ignoring me just as my father had. She used up too much energy handling the divorce and trying to support us to have time for me. I hardly saw her anymore. Some days she'd go out looking for work, while other times she'd just stay in bed crying. On those days she didn't even eat—she'd just bring a bottle up to the room and drink her meals.

"It was always worse just after she'd been in touch with my father for some reason. Most of the time he didn't send the money he was supposed to and he rarely came to see me. I remember wondering whether he didn't love me anymore or if he just didn't want to hear my mother yell at him. She'd begun doing that even when he wasn't there. She'd stand at the top of the stairs in her nightgown holding a drink and screaming about how my father was a no-good drunk.

"By my eleventh birthday, I'd still never had a drink, but before long I tried that amber-colored liquid that my parents relied on. It happened one day when I came home from school and no one was home. My mother had left me a note saying that she had to go out. I didn't know when she'd be back. I was hungry, but there was nothing to eat in the house. I didn't have any money or I'd have gone to Burger King or gotten a pizza or something.

"I waited for my mom until early evening before going to the liquor cabinet. Even though there wasn't any food, my mother kept her liquor supply in great shape. I picked out the prettiest bottle and poured some of it into a glass. Then I gulped it down the way my father did. It was awful. I hated the burning feeling it left in my mouth and throat.

"But even though it smarted going down, I think I realized why people drink. My whole body tingled and I felt comfortable and warm. I drank another glassful and fell asleep in the big chair in front of the television. I don't know what time my mother came home that night because I didn't wake up until the next morning.

"After that, drinking came easily for me. I'd secretly have a couple of drinks after school and again before bed to sleep better. This helped a lot because I'd been having bad dreams about never seeing my father again and I hated going to sleep.

"My mother was too overwhelmed by her own problems to even realize I was drinking. If she noticed the decrease in her liquor supply, she never mentioned it to me. But by then almost a year had passed, and I wasn't just drinking at home. Whenever I went to a party, I made sure to get my share of the booze or whatever other 'feel good' stuff was around. My girlfriend always teased me about it. She said that after she told me I looked glamorous with a drink in my hand, she never saw me at a party without one. I wanted to look good, but I also needed to drink. It helped me let go of my fears and feel popular.

"Being accepted and getting asked to go places was important to me. Most of the time I felt that my friends were all I had left. My father seemed to have disappeared from the face of the earth and after a while my mother found a boyfriend. He was younger than her and she slept at his place most nights instead of coming home. She'd usually leave me something to eat or money to buy food with. And there was always something to drink in the house, even if it were just beer or wine.

"Usually I got along okay by myself, but one night I just couldn't fall asleep. A horrible thunderstorm kept me up even after I'd had a few beers. When I was little I was terrified of thunder and I guess I never completely shook my fear.

"I wanted to sleep to escape the sound of the thunder. I knew my mother's doctor gave her sleeping pills to get through the divorce, but that she hadn't used them because they made her groggy. So I took two of them, hoping they'd do what the beer hadn't. But when I was still awake twenty minutes later, I took three more and washed them down with a couple of beers.

"I woke up in a hospital bed. I don't remember what happened, but I was told that my mother came home after she was unable to reach me by phone. When she couldn't wake me, she called the emergency medics. I don't know how long I was out, but when I opened my eyes, the doctor standing over me had said, 'Good morning young lady. Do you know that you're lucky to be alive?' "

◆ ◆ ◆ ◆

Thousands of miles away, Mike K., a freshman at a Boston area college had also been brought to a hospital in the early morning hours. Like Shannon he was there for an alcohol-related reason, although when Mike became intoxicated the previous night, he hadn't been depressed or frightened. He'd participated in a beer-guzzling contest at a fraternity party and had tried to outdrink his buddies at record speed. Although he left the party smashed, Mike doesn't know precisely when he passed out. He was only told that an ambulance was called after he was found unconscious, lying facedown in the street.

◆◆◆◆

While their circumstances differ, Shannon and Mike have a great deal in common with one another as well as with thousands of other American adolescents. At various times, scores of young adults have ended up in the hospital after consuming excessive quantities of alcohol. A study by Professor Henry Wechsler, of the Harvard School of Public Health, surveyed drinking habits among 1,600 freshmen at fourteen Massachusetts colleges. His research revealed that 92% of the males and 82% of the females regularly consumed a minimum of five consecutive drinks at parties or social gatherings where alcohol was available. Over half these students said that they drank to get drunk.[1]

Often the consequences of their intoxication have been potentially lethal or lethal. Medical personnel at the University of Massachusetts, as well as other educational institutions, report that over 80% of the student visits to

Here a group of students break the trend toward increasing alcohol and drug use by attending a rally to fight substance abuse.

local health services and hospitals are alcohol-related. As one Mount Holyoke student alcohol counselor described the situation, "You see the ambulances on college campuses all the time."[2]

In the worst scenarios, young people actually die of alcohol poisoning. That's what happened to an eighteen-year-old Rutgers University student who was forced to drink excessively while pledging for a college fraternity. In another instance, thirty-nine fraternity pledges at Princeton University wound up at the school infirmary and local hospital after having been led blindfolded through an initiation ceremony in which liquor was poured down their throats. One of the students remained in a coma for over twenty-four hours.

Authorities report that raising the legal drinking age has not helped the situation. A recent survey of seventy-six New York state colleges and universities demonstrated that the percentage of serious campus drinking problems actually rose from 38% to 43% when the state drinking age was raised from eighteen to twenty-one. On a national level, approximately 40% of all college students go on drinking binges at least once every two weeks, while nearly 4%, about one-half million, drink daily.[3]

In addition, other indicators show that drinking is also prevalent among American youths long before they reach college age. Twenty-six percent of today's fourth graders and 42% of sixth graders have already used alcohol. The most commonly cited reasons given by elementary school students for drinking include the desire to "fit in with others" as well as a need "to feel older."

Alcohol use substantially increases in junior and senior high school. Nearly 90% of tenth graders in the United States have tried alcohol at least once, while six out of every ten high school seniors regularly use alcohol. Thirty percent of these students had five or more drinks in a row within the previous two weeks.[4]

Teenagers often find alcoholic beverages available to them at unsupervised parties and at their friends' homes. And many habitually skirt state minimum-age purchase laws by having an older friend buy the beer or liquor for them. In other instances, they patronize establishments known not to question youthful customers about their age. One study on the accessibility of alcohol to young people revealed that older teens in the Washington, D.C., area who attempted to purchase alcoholic beverages were successful 97 out of 100 times. In similar research conducted in Westchester County, New York, the young people succeeded 80% of the time.[5] Many teens report that false IDs, which are used to buy liquor or enter establishments where liquor is served, are fairly easy to obtain.

It's significantly more difficult for grade school and

junior high students to purchase alcohol. But, treatment centers report that these young people frequently get it by stealing liquor, wine, and beer from their parents' household supply. Many young people who drink do so knowing very little about the consequences of their actions. A survey conducted by the Inspector General revealed that 5.6 million teens aren't aware that the minimum legal drinking age is twenty-one in all fifty states. Perhaps even more alarming is the fact that over two million young adults don't even know that such laws exist.[6]

Because it can be purchased legally by adults, alcohol may not be readily thought of as a drug. Another government study revealed that a third of American teens wrongfully believe that drinking coffee, taking a cold shower, or getting some fresh air can adequately "sober you up."

Effects and Risks of Alcohol Use

Alcohol is sometimes called a "downer" because it acts to depress the central nervous system. Once swallowed, it is absorbed into the bloodstream and transported throughout the body. After drinking a moderate amount of alcohol, an individual may experience flushing, dizziness, and dulled senses, as well as impaired coordination, reflexes, memory, and judgment. Larger amounts can cause staggering, slurred speech, double vision, sudden mood changes, and even unconsciousness.

Alcohol affects almost every organ system, either directly or indirectly. Some of the ways it assaults the body are listed below:

- ✔ Liver. Heavy drinking for an extended period of time may result in cirrhosis, a disease that damages the liver.

- ✔ Heart. Alcohol places an added strain on the heart, causing it to pump harder. Excessive chronic alcohol use has frequently left drinkers with an irregular heartbeat, as well as high blood pressure.

- ✔ Stomach. Alcohol takes its toll on the digestive system, including the stomach. At times, stomach ulcers may develop due to persistent use of alcohol.

- ✔ Kidneys. Alcohol can disrupt normal kidney functioning. This disturbance also can have a negative effect on related organs.

- ✔ Mouth and Throat. Alcohol irritates the lining of the drinker's mouth and throat. With ongoing heavy use, this irritation produces discomfort as well as painful sores.

- ✔ Pregnancy. A pregnant woman who drinks may give birth to an infant with fetal alcohol syndrome. This irreversible condition can cause mental retardation or learning disabilities, distorted facial features, malformed organs, behavioral problems and poor coordination.

Individuals who drink excessively for extended periods may suffer from a condition known as the DTs, or delirium tremens, when they try to stop. The DTs can result in mental turmoil, extreme shaking and trembling, terrifying hallucinations, and in some cases even death. Still another possible consequence of heavy chronic drinking is Korsakoff's syndrome, which is similar to the DTs. Korsakoff's syndrome may produce mental disorientation and hallucinations. However, it can also result in paralysis of the hands and feet.

Considerable alcohol use may also lead to malnutrition, lowered resistance to disease and irreversible brain or nervous system damage. People who both smoke and drink are at a greater risk of developing certain types of cancer as well. In time, alcohol use may even result in physical dependence on the drug. At that point, the addicted person may need increasing levels of alcohol just to get through the day.

How a person responds to alcohol depends on the quantity of alcohol consumed, the amount of food eaten prior to drinking, how quickly the alcohol was ingested as well as the person's mood, weight and prior drinking experience. If combined with tranquilizers, sleeping pills, marijuana, or antihistamines, a significantly lesser amount of alcohol can be fatal.

Special Risks for Teenage Drinkers

Unfortunately, alcohol poses some special risks for youths. Since young people tend to have a lower alcohol tolerance than adults, the same amount of alcohol will usually affect an adolescent more severely than an older person. Alcohol has also been identified as a "gateway drug," which is a substance that can lead to abuse of more harmful drugs. In other words, someone who uses alcohol at an early age is more likely to drink heavily later on or abuse other drugs.

Excessive alcohol use generally cannot be separated from other facets of a young person's life. Alcohol abuse has been associated with a host of problems, often including poor academic performance, truancy and juvenile crime. As young people become more heavily involved with alcohol, they are often distracted from the normal school and social pursuits that might have formerly characterized their life.

This becomes especially evident as the heavy-drinking teen finds it necessary to drink increasing amounts of alcohol in order to maintain the desired effect. Such individuals usually start their day with a drink and then spend the rest of their waking hours trying to secure the alcohol they now desperately need. Because they frequently lack the funds to purchase these beverages, as well as being too young to legally consume them, their efforts to obtain alcohol can go from encounters with friends and school faculty members to even less pleasant interactions with the police. As alcohol robs these young people of what they were, they may become like strangers to those who've known and cared for them all their lives.

Some teenagers think they can avoid these negative consequences by drinking what they believe are milder alcoholic beverages. But a 12-ounce can of beer contains as much alcohol as a shot of whiskey or a 5-ounce glass of wine. A recent study demonstrated that delaying an individual's initial use of alcohol to some time beyond childhood and adolescence greatly reduces his or her risk of adult alcohol and drug problems. Yet, unfortunately, alcohol remains the drug most commonly abused by America's youth.

2

Drinking and Driving

Kim (age 18)

"I wanted to go out with Eric for as long as I can remember. He had everything—he was good-looking, into body-building, and on the football team. I always thought of him as the kind of guy you'd see in a movie magazine and I think most girls would agree with me.

"Eric never asked me out. I didn't really expect him to because he was someone you dreamed about rather than really dated. But whenever I could, I tried to be where he was. I'd root for him at football games, talk to him after class and at parties, and watch him drag-race with his friends.

"Eric won the races most of the time. He had great coordination and was a terrific driver. Sometimes the guys raced their cars after having a few beers. We all knew that you're not supposed to drink and drive. But nobody ever paid that any mind. Eric always said those warnings applied to old people, not athletes like himself.

"I thought he was right. Eric drank and drove whenever it suited him and nothing ever happened. In fact, he was sober the only time he was ever stopped for speeding.

"Eric could do sharp curves at high speed with one hand on the wheel and a beer in the other. He'd drive a group of us to the pizza place or to a party when he was high, but I never thought twice about riding with him. Eric seemed invincible, nothing bad could happen to someone like him.

"If a group of us were heading someplace, I'd usually go in Eric's car. It was fun to be with him and the people he hung out with. I was proud to be one of them. That's why I was really pissed the Friday after graduation when a bunch of us decided to leave one party to go to another at the beach. I just assumed that I'd be in Eric's car, but three other girls asked him for a ride before I could. I knew the girls from school and even though they were friends, any of them would have been thrilled if Eric asked her out. Between the three of them and his two best friends from the football team, there wasn't any room left in the car for me.

"Getting a ride to the beach that night wasn't really a problem because other kids with cars were going too. I just hated the idea of being left out. I ended up going with my best friend, her boyfriend, and a couple of other kids I didn't know that well.

"The party was okay. I met a guy going to the same college that I was going to in the fall and we compared notes on what we knew about the place. When Eric and the kids he left with didn't show up, I figured that they went somewhere else at the last minute.

"I found out what really happened the next day, but I didn't believe it at first. I thought that maybe there was some mistake—that somehow the names had been mixed up or something. But I couldn't deny the truth for long. I knew that I'd be going to a funeral soon. Eric had crashed the car on the way to the beach. Everyone in the collision had been hurt and two of the girls who'd asked Eric for a ride were dead.

"I felt guilty for having begrudged them the ride that killed them. I couldn't stop thinking about how much I had wanted to be in their place that night. The police report showed that Eric was drunk at the time of the accident. Suddenly he didn't seem invincible any longer—now he seemed like a murderer. And I knew that I could easily have been one of his victims."

◆ ◆ ◆ ◆

Stories such as Kim's are not unusual. The tragedy of teen drinking and driving has become all too familiar in

Fatal head-on collisions are a common and deadly consequence of drunk driving.

households across the country. As in the case of Eric and his friends, drunken driving has destroyed the lives of numerous American teens. It happened to Mark Hier, a seemingly gifted young man who graduated as his school's valedictorian and went on to study engineering at Rensselaer Polytechnic Institute in Troy, New York.

Initially, Mark did well in college, but after he started drinking regularly with his fraternity friends, his grades began to slip. Then on March 3, 1989, he left a fraternity beer party with two friends to go to another beer blast. Like Eric, most of the people at the party had been drinking, including the young man driving Mark and his friend to their next stop. Unfortunately, the three never reached it. The intoxicated driver steered the car into a pole. Both Mark and the other passenger were killed.

Michael von Ruecker of Clayton, Missouri, is a third example of the perilous consequences of drunk driving. At nineteen, Michael was thrilled to have found a bar where IDs weren't checked. One evening he had a number of drinks there before heading home in his car. The next day he lay paralyzed in the hospital.

Michael von Ruecker survived his automobile accident but was left a quadriplegic—he only has limited movement in one arm. Determined to go on with his life—now vastly different from what he had planned—Michael attended the University of Missouri in a

A police officer, who has seen first-hand that alcohol and gasoline don't mix, lectures a class on the dangers of substance abuse.

wheelchair. His fellow students helped him to dress each day and perform other simple tasks. Like other young people who think drinking is just harmless fun, Mike says he never dreamed that something like this could happen to him—yet it did.

Sadly, over twice as many young licensed drivers are involved in alcohol-related car accidents than drivers over thirty.[1] And while the number of teen drunken driving fatalities has statistically decreased somewhat since 1982, young people are still over-represented in this category.

Often, teenagers base their decision to drink and drive on misinformation. Since alcohol may produce temporary feelings of euphoria, some teen drivers mistakenly believe that their driving skills are actually enhanced after a few drinks. But nothing could be further from the truth. Instead, alcohol dulls areas of the brain crucial to roadway decision making, decreases the ability to concentrate, and slows reaction time behind the wheel. Drunk drivers may also experience blurred or double vision, making them even more treacherous on the road.

Driving while intoxicated is against the law in every state. Law enforcement authorities generally determine if a driver is guilty of driving while intoxicated (DWI) by the amount of alcohol in his or her "blood alcohol concentration" (BAC) (see Chart 1). This information may be ascertained either through a breath tester, for which

ENJOY YOUR BEVERAGE, BUT
KNOW YOUR LIMITS

CHART FOR RESPONSIBLE PEOPLE WHO MAY SOMETIMES DRIVE AFTER DRINKING

APPROXIMATE BLOOD ALCOHOL PERCENTAGE

Drinks	Body Weight in Pounds								
	100	120	140	160	180	200	220	240	
1	.04	.03	.03	.02	.02	.02	.02	.02	Rarely Influenced
2	.08	.06	.05	.05	.04	.04	.03	.03	
3	.11	.09	.08	.07	.06	.06	.05	.05	Possibly
4	.15	.12	.11	.09	.08	.08	.07	.06	
5	.19	.16	.13	.12	.11	.09	.09	.08	
6	.23	.19	.16	.14	.13	.11	.10	.09	
7	.26	.22	.19	.16	.15	.13	.12	.11	Definitely (Unlawful to Drive)
8	.30	.25	.21	.19	.17	.15	.14	.13	
9	.34	.28	.24	.21	.19	.17	.15	.14	
10	.38	.31	.27	.23	.21	.19	.17	.16	

Subtract .01 for each 40 minutes of drinking.
One drink is 1 oz. of 80 proof liquor, 12 oz. of beer, 4 oz. of table wine.

THE FIRST ABC OF THE ROAD—DRIVE SOBER

the driver is asked to breathe into a device, or by direct analysis of the person's blood or urine.

Most states have laws indicating that any driver with a blood alcohol concentration of 0.10% or more is legally intoxicated. In some parts of the country, drivers with a BAC of between 0.05 and 0.10% can be convicted of a lesser alcohol-related charge. Twenty-nine states and the District of Columbia permit an individual's driver's license to be automatically suspended or revoked for operating a vehicle at or above a specific blood alcohol level.

Some states have gone one step farther. These have established lower legal BAC levels and specialized penalties for youthful offenders. They are as follows:

• *Arizona* (BAC level = 0.00). It's a misdemeanor for a minor to drive with any trace of alcohol in his blood. However, if the individual's BAC level is less than 0.10 his license may or may not automatically be suspended or revoked.

• *California* (BAC level = 0.05). Drivers under eighteen with a BAC level at or above 0.05 are considered guilty of a Special Juvenile Offense. They may be subject to either a sentence of community service work or attending an alcohol education program.

• *Georgia* (BAC level = 0.06). Any driver under eighteen who has a BAC at or above 0.06 is deemed DWI.

• *Maine* (BAC level = 0.02). Those drivers under twenty-one who have a BAC at or above 0.02 may have their licenses automatically suspended.

• *Maryland* (BAC level = 0.02). Drivers under twenty-one are prohibited from operating a motor vehicle when they have a BAC level at or above 0.02.

• *New Mexico* (BAC level = 0.05). Minors showing a BAC level at or above 0.05 when stopped by police may have their driving privileges revoked.

• *North Carolina* (BAC level = 0.00). Drivers under nineteen found to have any level of alcohol in their blood may have their driving privileges automatically revoked.

• *Ohio* (BAC level = 0.02). Drivers under eighteen having a BAC level at or above 0.02 may have their driving privileges suspended.

• *Oregon* (BAC level = 0.00). Drivers under twenty-one with any trace of alcohol in their bloodstream may have their driving privileges suspended.

• *Rhode Island* (BAC level = 0.04). Drivers under eighteen found to have a BAC at or above 0.04 may be subjected to special licensing restrictions, community service work and fines.

• *Vermont* (BAC level = 0.02). Drivers under eighteen found to have a BAC level at or above 0.02 may have their licenses suspended as well as be required to attend an alcohol education program or therapy sessions.

• *Wisconsin* (BAC level = 0.00). Drivers under eighteen may have their license suspended or revoked if they are found to have any trace of alcohol in their blood.

After conducting a series of public hearings in the late 1980s to learn more about intoxicated teen drivers, the National Commission Against Drunk Driving recommended that the BAC level for minors be nationally set at 0.00 percent. This would mean that a driver under twenty-one with even the slightest trace of alcohol in his blood would be considered DWI.

Besides legislative efforts to reduce drunk driving, various civic and community groups have formed to combat the problem as well. Among these is Students Against Drunk Driving (S.A.D.D.), a nationwide student organization dedicated to combating teen drinking and driving. These students strive to educate other young people about the negative consequences of drunk driving. In addition to their numerous other activities, they sponsor anti-alcohol-abuse peer counseling as well as work to increase general public awareness of, and prevention of, the problem.

The "Contract for Life Between Parent and Teenager" distributed by S.A.D.D. is among the group's most valuable lifesaving measures. Under this agreement, signed by both the teenager and parent, the young person

S.A.D.D. members from Deer Valley High School in Phoenix, Arizona, proudly display a banner bearing the group's slogan.

agrees to call home "for advice and/or transportation at any hour from any place," if he finds himself in "a situation where a driver has been drinking or using illicit drugs." In turn, the parent agrees to either pick up the young person at "any place, no questions asked and no argument at that time" or "pay for a taxi" to bring the teen home safely.

Another teen program making a life-and-death difference is Teen Saferides. This group relies on the volunteer efforts of sober, reliable teens to safely drive home intoxicated young people or those who face either being stranded somewhere or going home with an intoxicated driver.

Often Saferide volunteers equip themselves with an emergency kit containing a walkie-talkie, first aid supplies, a fire extinguisher, maps, a flashlight, flares, and even airsickness bags. Some Teen Saferide centers operate between 10 P.M. and 2 A.M. on Friday and Saturday nights, and frequently find that they are most busy on holiday weekends, New Year's Eve, and prom nights. The volunteers generally work in pairs on four-hour shifts and are supervised by adults.

Mothers Against Drunk Driving (M.A.D.D.) is a national organization that defines its "mission" as: "to stop drunk driving and to support the victims of violent crimes." At times the group has aimed its efforts at teenagers, and various M.A.D.D. chapters have accomplished some inspiring goals. Georgia's Dougherty/Lee counties chapter significantly enhanced public awareness regarding drunk driving through its creation of a "Red Ribbon Mile of Hope." During National Drunk and Drugged Driving Awareness Week, a group of the chapter's "M.A.D.D. Dads" put up 200 wooden posts at an intersection where numerous fatalities had occurred. The effect was heightened as additional M.A.D.D. members tied red bows to each post and placed a mile of red ribbon along both sides of the road.

To intensify legal efforts to combat drunk driving, M.A.D.D.'s New Mexico chapter sent Christmas cards containing a wish list to every member of the state legislature as well as to local judges and city officials. The list emphasized stiffer anti-drunk-driving laws, which the group hoped would be adopted during the upcoming legislative session.

In addition to these and other valuable volunteer efforts, many school systems and social organizations now sponsor teen chemical-free graduation parties, senior trips and carnivals. The concept of drug- and alcohol-free teen celebrations is not new—numerous Oregon high schools have sponsored alcohol-free graduation parties for over forty years. However, the idea became increasingly popular in the 1980s after a total of eighteen people in Maine

Sparta High School students in Sparta, New Jersey, prepare for an alcohol- and drug-free celebration.

were killed in alcohol-related car crashes during two consecutive graduation seasons.

Alcohol-free social events are a way for teens who respect life to start a new national tradition. It's a challenging, but possible goal. As the S.A.D.D. slogan states: "If We Dream It, It Can Be Done." [2]

3

Young Drinkers

Brian (age 17)

"As a little kid, I used to wander around the living room taking sips from my father's and uncle's beers. My mother would tell me to stop, but Dad always overruled her. He'd just chuckle and proudly say, 'The boy's growing up. Before you know it our little one will be a man.'

"Wanting to please my father and live up to his expectations, I made a habit of openly stealing swallows from his beer whenever he and my uncle watched the Sunday TV ball games. I was just six years old back then but I drank to get my Dad's approval. By the time I was a sophomore in high school, I'd down a six-pack in an evening and do my best to hide it from my father."

◆ ◆ ◆ ◆

It's impossible to categorize the typical teenage drinker.

Teens use alcohol for a wide variety of reasons, and they demonstrate considerable differences in drinking patterns. How much and how often alcohol is consumed largely depends on the individual. However, the following causes for teen alcohol abuse are among those most frequently cited.

Societal Influences

Alcohol use is extremely prevalent in our society. Young people grow up seeing their parents and other adults make toasts at weddings and anniversaries with a glass of champagne, as well as casually enjoy a few beers or wine at a family picnic. Alcoholic beverages are frequently as common at business lunches as they are at college fraternity parties.

Actually, our country has a long history of alcohol use. In 1609, just two years after the first English colonists arrived at Jamestown, the settlers ran an advertisement in a London newspaper for a brewer to come to the colony. However, it was the Dutch who, after settling in New York, established the first distillery in the New World in 1640.

During the 1600s and 1700s, colonists regularly consumed ample quantities of beer, rum, wine and alcohol-based cider. It is estimated that the average colonist annually drank the equivalent of thirty-nine gallons of

Unfortunately, alcohol use is prevalent at all levels of society. Here a traditional New Year's Eve champagne toast has been poured.

wine or seventy gallons of beer. Often their alcohol intake was a matter of practicality; coffee and tea were highly priced, and the water and available unpasteurized milk were frequently contaminated.

As time passed, increasing numbers of immigrants from various countries arrived in America. Among these were Irish and Scottish settlers who brought the whiskey-distilling techniques of their homelands to their new country. Brewing and enjoying spirits came to be accepted as a part of American life and were regarded as basic rights.

These feelings were behind the Whiskey Rebellion of 1794, during which Pennsylvania distillers tried to resist a government tax on whiskey. Although the revolt was unsuccessful, it underscored the popular belief that Americans had the right to distill and drink whiskey without penalty. A similar stance was taken in what is now Kentucky when in 1810 tax collectors found it impossible to collect revenues from the owners of over 2,000 breweries who objected to additional whiskey taxes.

However, not everyone was enthusiastic about the high level of alcohol consumption among Americans. Physicians were concerned about the negative health aspects associated with excessive drinking, while religious leaders worried about the moral lapses alcohol consumption could lead to. Individuals, hoping to lessen or even eliminate the availability of alcohol, joined together to form the temperance movement. During the 1850s, pressure from temperance activists resulted in nearly a dozen states going "dry" or outlawing alcoholic beverages.

As time passed the temperance movement gained momentum and by 1869 the Prohibition Party, which sponsored anti-alcohol candidates for public office, was established. Five years later in 1874, a group of religious women concerned about the evils of alcohol founded the Woman's Christian Temperance Union (WCTU). The WCTU continually urged habitual drinkers to reform as well as encouraged public officials to ban the sale of alcohol throughout the nation. Proponents of the temperance movement argued that alcohol was responsible for the social and moral breakdown in America and stressed that American industry would also profit from increased productivity if alcohol was not readily available to workers.

Before long, an increasing number of states and localities passed ordinances to prohibit the sale and use of alcohol. However, the temperance movement continued to seek more sweeping changes. They petitioned elected representatives to sponsor a constitutional amendment to limit alcohol's availability. Their hopes were realized in January 1919 when the Eighteenth Amendment to the

U.S. Constitution was ratified, outlawing the production, sale and distribution of alcoholic beverages.

Although Prohibition made liquor more costly and difficult to come by, it did not stop its flow. A sizable number of Americans refused to give up alcohol and were willing to break the law to secure it. In some parts of the country, people made liquor in small stills they kept hidden on their property. Others drank in secretly-run nightclubs called speakeasies. The demand for the now-illegal liquid was often met by people called bootleggers who distributed the banned alcohol and sometimes had ties to organized crime. Since there was a great deal of money to be made smuggling liquor into the United States from Canada and other locations, gang wars over sales turf were not uncommon during this period.

Prohibition did not turn America into a "dry" country as intended. Instead, flagrant violations of the law were so widespread that it was impossible to effectively enforce existing regulations. As a result, the Eighteenth Amendment was repealed on December 5, 1933. Prohibition made it exceedingly clear that Americans would not tolerate the government telling them they couldn't drink. Alcohol had become an ingrained aspect of America's culture.

To some degree this attitude persists today among college students who habitually drink. Many young people have come to regard alcohol as an important and often necessary vehicle for relaxation and socializing. When asked why they drank at parties, a significant number noted that alcohol made them "feel free" or afforded them the chance to be themselves. The following remarks by a college student for a television documentary on campus drinking are considered typical of the feelings often expressed by young binge drinkers. He stated:

> After you have a few beers, you're just like, "Hey, I'm rolling, I'm having a good time, and I'm not, you know, going to worry about anything else. . . . I prefer drinking in excess, I suppose—let's say ten [drinks]—just 'cause it seems like whenever I go over the limit, then you just—you're so free, you're just having the best time, you don't have a care in the world. And it seems like most of my good times drinking come after, you know, eight, nine, ten beers, rather than just two.[1]

A female student at the same school described how alcohol lowers her inhibitions in social situations:

> You just talk—start talking to people and you don't care what they think about you. And you don't—I mean, I don't even bother reapplying lipstick or going to the bathroom to check my hair anymore, you know. . . . You don't realize you're drinking so much and by the end of the night, you don't remember anything. The next day, you're like, "I did that?"[2]

At some colleges and universities, standard party behavior often includes drinking rituals. As Carl Wurtenberg, alcohol abuse expert, described this phenomenon, "There's an intensity about it. There's a frequency that's much increased. . . . Now the object of the evening [is] 'Let's go get blitzed. Let's get wasted, let's get ripped.' "[3]

One of the ways to drink alcohol at some college parties is through a process known as shotgunning. This technique involves opening the top of a beer can as well as punching a hole in its bottom to suck the beer out. The idea is to ingest as much alcohol as possible in the shortest amount of time. Another party alternative is keg-standing. Here the young person is held upside down by his friends while drinking beer through a hose. Those who prefer eating their alcohol may fill up on Jell-O shots—a concoction of largely Jell-O and alcohol. One partygoer described the appeal of these unorthodox snacks, "You suck it right out of the cup. It's beautiful."

Do these students really need to drink as much as they do in order to enjoy themselves? The psychological draw of alcohol was especially evident during a study at the Addictive Behaviors Research Center at the University of Washington in Seattle. A research scientist at the Center told student volunteers that they would be served drinks for about forty minutes and questioned afterward about the alcohol's effects. In each group of participants, about half the students said that the alcohol had taken its toll on them. Their responses were often similar to the sampling quoted below:

First student: "[I feel] sleepy. . . . I always fall asleep when I drink."

Second student: "When we stand up we're going to be really feeling it. . . . My legs feel funny . . . ." [4]

A large number of students reported that the alcohol made them feel "woozy," "sleepy," or "happy."

However, before the students left, the research scientist revealed the truth about what had actually taken place. He told them, "None of the beverages you consumed tonight had any alcohol in them. . . . So you see, it isn't just the beverage, it's your psychological set or your expectations and the setting you're in. So it may be that the alcohol doesn't make the party. It may be that you and your friends make the party." [5]

Yet, despite such revealing insights, recent surveys indicate that on most college campuses across the country a sizable number of students continue to go on drinking binges.

Media Influences

Alcohol's appeal to teens is further enhanced by advertising and marketing efforts primarily aimed at

Combating the image of sports figures who endorse alcoholic beverages, Paul Silas of the Boston Celtics cautions teens against using alcohol.

young people. The National Council on Alcoholism believes that American youths view approximately one hundred thousand beer commercials before they turn eighteen. Even though a number of professional athletes have made the evening news after being picked up for drunk driving, sports stars still appear in TV commercials praising various beers and malt liquors. The vast majority of sporting events, including basketball games, triathalons, and tennis matches, are largely sponsored by brewers and distillers.

Unfortunately, the association between athletes and drinking is so firmly implanted in people's minds that many teens assume that sports figures drink heavily at parties and social events without it affecting their ability and performance. In actuality, this is merely a perception carefully crafted by the media. For example, while the U.S. Olympic Committee's Sports Medicine Council continues to discourage alcohol use for Olympic athletes, much of the 1992 Summer Olympics television coverage was nevertheless sponsored by beer companies.

Even the advertisements for alcoholic beverages that don't feature sports figures promote the image of a fantasy life enhanced by the glow of beer or liquor. The dog Spuds MacKenzie, formerly shown in a number of beer commercials, was also marketed as a stuffed toy for children. Apparently, media consultants have been

Spuds MacKenzie may be a Bud Lite mascot, but a fifth-grade class drew Garfield the cat to remind others to steer clear of alcohol and other drugs.

extremely successful at reaching increasingly younger age groups. A government study on youth and alcohol revealed that 39% of the teens and preteens surveyed were able to precisely pinpoint some aspect of the liquor ads that they found especially appealing. Their reactions were summarized as follows:

> They said that ads made drinking look glamorous and fun. Specifically, they mentioned that the ads had sexy people in them. They mentioned things like, "makes you look like you're accepted" and that "the girls in the ads are skinny and I want to look like that." Also more than half the students knew that Spuds MacKenzie was not a Coors mascot but a Bud Lite mascot. A fact that tells that the ads may be a stronger influence on students than they realize.[6]

Under the circumstances, it is not surprising that many young people think of alcohol use as an initiation into adulthood. While the majority of teens may experiment with alcohol at least once or twice before reaching the legal drinking age, in some instances such experimentation leads to serious alcohol abuse.

Family Lifestyle

In many instances, drinking problems within the home, a family crisis, or merely the way family members relate to one another can influence a teenager's drinking. Divorce as well as spouse and child abuse are common factors frequently associated with teen alcohol and drug abuse. The death of a parent or sibling has also been known to spark drinking bouts.

Some teens respond to parental pressure by drinking. It is often their way of coping with an intensely competitive sibling situation or a parent's wish that they be admitted to a particular college or make a school athletic team.

Teenagers are also often influenced by how those around them use alcohol. A parent who habitually has several cocktails before dinner implies that drinking regularly is acceptable and appropriate. Though parents may lecture their children on alcohol's negative effects and encourage them not to drink, actions tend to speak louder than words.

At times, alcoholic parents, so that they can secretly drink, have enrolled their children in a wide range of after-school activities or put them to bed early. The children are supposedly unaware of the parent's ploy, but they usually discover what's happening before too long. Other parents, who feel guilty about the toll their drinking takes on the family, may try to spoil their children by purchasing an assortment of high-tech electronic toys or designer outfits for them. Although such material trophies have their appeal, often the young people would prefer having a parent who spends time with them and is emotionally there for them.

A recovering alcoholic mother described what growing up with a parent who drinks too much can be like:

> In the alcoholic's family, the broken promises are endless. The price the other family members pay is enormous, but because many are used to the situation, they don't even realize how great it is. As long as there's abusive drinking, the liquor and not the family will be the number-one priority.[7]

While the young people may abhor the drinking habits of their parents, they may eventually turn to alcohol to handle their problems and anguish as well. Children learn through example, and in many instances these young people never saw healthier ways to cope with their problems.

Research has shown that 80% of the families in which both parents drink produce children who drink, while 70% of families in which neither parent drinks have offspring who don't use alcohol.[8]

Predisposition to Alcohol

Some individuals are more likely than others to become addicted to alcohol due to factors in their physical makeup. Heredity and genetics cannot be ignored in exploring the causes of alcohol abuse. Accessing knowledge of the degree of alcohol addiction in a teen's immediate and extended family can be vital in learning if he is predisposed to become an alcoholic.

Studies indicate that about half the children of alcoholic parents will become alcoholics themselves.[9] Often these teens become "hooked" after just a few drinking bouts and report that for them, alcohol almost immediately produces a sense of extreme well-being, joy and relief from anxiety. It is especially important for young people predisposed to alcoholism to completely abstain from alcohol consumption.

Peer Group Pressure

During adolescence a young person's need to be accepted by his friends and classmates often becomes paramount. If drinking is necessary "to fit in" with the others, many young people will do what's expected of them, whether or not they even enjoy drinking. As one fifteen-year-old put it, "I don't really like to drink. I never got used to the taste and I know that stuff is fattening. But when I go to parties I drink—I do it to be like everybody else. If I didn't, I'm not sure that I'd keep on being invited."

In some social circles, peer pressure on teenage boys to drink can be even more intense. At times getting drunk may be viewed as both a rite of passage into adulthood and a reflection of a young man's masculinity. Boys who refuse to drink may be teased, excluded and perceived as weaklings.

Adolescent Turmoil

The teen years are frequently characterized by conflict and stress. Teens must make the transition from childhood to young adulthood, but to do so they need to learn a wide variety of new intellectual and social skills. Struggling to adequately function in their new roles, many teens turn to alcohol to help them handle stressful situations.

Adolescence is also a time of rebellion. Teenagers begin to separate from their parents, to establish unique identities of their own. Drinking, staying out late and "breaking all the rules," are often symbolic of this rebellious stage.

Serious Psychological and Emotional Problems

Teens suffering from psychological and emotional problems may be among those most likely to use alcohol. Feeling overwhelmed in their everyday lives, they frequently experience anxiety, depression, and confusion, as well as feelings of disorganization and helplessness. At first young people may rely on alcohol to numb their pain, but if they continue to use alcohol, before long they will face a whole new set of problems resulting from substance abuse.

Although the factors described above frequently play a role in teen alcohol use, substance abuse is a complicated problem that can never be adequately understood by isolating a single cause. Instead, it usually results from a number of these aspects interacting with one another. Each case of teen substance abuse is unique and must always be seen as such.

4

Seeing the Signs

Greg (age 15)

"After our father died, my older brother Mike and I were together more often. Now he didn't tease me the way he used to and he stopped treating me like a little kid. Sometimes Mike even let me hang out with him and his friends. Our Mom depended on Mike more too. He took over most of the chores our father did around the house, and I knew that Mom discussed important decisions with him.

"But that was before our mother remarried and everything changed. Our new stepfather was Mr. Burns, the physical education coach at the junior high. I don't think I ever saw Mr. Burns at school without a whistle in his mouth. He liked being in charge and giving orders, and he was the same way at home with us. It was like Mike and I were suddenly back in kindergarten.

"Mom never asked Mike about stuff anymore. She sided with Mr. Burns on everything and kept telling us to try harder to please him. She wanted him to be our new father, but he could never replace our Dad.

"I think Mike took it worse than me because he was older and had liked being the man of the house. He started spending more time in his room with the door locked. Mr. Burns sent him to his room so often that I think this was Mike's way of beating our stepfather to the punch.

"Everyday after school Mike would race upstairs to his room and blast his stereo. I saw that my brother was changing. He avoided me, his friends at school, and even lost interest in sports. Most of the time he didn't even eat dinner with us, but would sneak downstairs later to bring something to his room. Mike wanted everyone to think he was starving, but we all knew that he was eating up there. Still it wasn't until much later than we learned he was also drinking behind his locked door."

◆ ◆ ◆ ◆

Situations similar to Mike's are not uncommon among juvenile drinkers. Since teens who drink heavily in response to a crisis often do so in isolation, it's useful to know the typical warning signs of a young person involved in substance abuse.

Warning Signs of Substance Abuse

Distancing Themselves from Family Members and Friends. Teens who suddenly go out of their way to avoid friends and loved ones they were formerly close to are often displaying one of the early signs of alcohol abuse. The process may start with the young person continually excusing himself from family activities such as picnics, holiday celebrations, church functions and camping trips.

While the youth may now spend more time alone than ever before, he or she will also begin to emotionally distance himself or herself. Many of these young people wear earphones and continually listen to music tapes to effectively block everyone else out. They frequently also claim that they aren't hungry at meal times so as not to have to eat with the rest of the family.

Behavioral Changes at School. Teen alcohol abuse generally affects a young person's behavior and takes a toll on school performance. In the majority of cases, there's a significant rise in absenteeism, with some students staying out two and three days at a time. These teens also tend to cut classes—especially when a quiz or test is scheduled. As might be expected, their grades

Phil Buckman (Slash of "Drexell's Class") speaks to students at Eaton Rapids High School in Michigan. These school programs reach out to students who may be grappling with substance abuse.

usually fall. Some students who never received less than a B will now both fail some courses and get low marks in others.

Teens with serious drinking problems also often lose interest in extracurricular activities. Outstanding athletes refuse to try out for teams, just as formerly promising would-be scientists and engineers no longer participate in school science fairs. These students now spend most of their time securing and drinking significant quantities of alcohol. Everything else becomes secondary as the alcohol they consume begins to consumes them.

Before long, it becomes increasingly difficult for teen problem drinkers to function at all in school. Hostile confrontations erupt between them and the administration over incomplete assignments, excessive absenteeism, truancy and bringing alcohol to school.

If these students don't receive help from a guidance counselor, school nurse, social worker, or other responsible adult before the situation further deteriorates, many will drop out of school.

Such young people usually alienate their former friends as well. The friends often become impatient with the drinker's isolation tactics, his or her lack of concern about their needs and feelings and inappropriate behavior both in and out of school. While some may initially reach out to help their friend, after a time, others will just ignore him.

New Social Interactions. As the teen problem drinker increasingly withdraws from family and friends, he or she may begin to form new relationships with somewhat older individuals who are also involved in substance abuse. Their recreational activities often largely center around drugs and alcohol and may include all-night parties, drinking contests, rock concerts and casual sex. Unfortunately, the drinker's new friends become a barrier to positive life-style changes, since their values and actions serve to reinforce the troubled teen's self-destructive behavior.

Physical Symptoms. Once the teenager's life is firmly centered around alcohol use, numerous undesirable physical symptoms appear. These sometimes include hangovers, exhaustion, depression, blackouts and irrational thinking. In many ways, his entire personality may seem to dramatically change. Some teen heavy drinkers expose themselves to injury and pain by putting out lit cigarettes on their arms and various other parts of their bodies. Numerous youthful drinkers habitually become involved in fights with little provocation and may curse and degrade their parents in arguments. Others acquire a history of suicide attempts.

At first it may be difficult to recognize and come to terms with the signs of substance abuse in a friend, sibling, or even yourself. To some degree every individual responds uniquely to alcohol. Although it may be painful to admit that you or someone close to you is out of control, it is necessary to do so before positive intervention and treatment can occur.

5

The Family Response

Mrs. K.

"I guess I saw the signs of my daughter's drinking problem fairly soon, but I just didn't have the strength to admit it. If Tracy were abusing alcohol and drugs, then what kind of a mother did that make me? I gave up a promising advertising career so I could stay home and raise her properly, and I guess I don't have much to show for it today.

"When Tracy was in grade school and junior high she was the joy of our lives. Her father and I couldn't have been prouder of her. We'd been blessed with a daughter who had good looks, good health and a wonderful mind. She raised tropical fish and wanted to study oceanography when she went to college.

"But after she started dating her boyfriend Gary

everything changed. My husband and I both felt that Gary was too old for our daughter, but Tracy refused to listen to us. In her mind, Gary represented everything that was hip and desirable. He was the boy she wanted to be with and she referred to her old values as kid stuff. I guess Tracy thought she didn't need her parents anymore. She rarely did things with us and stopped telling us her thoughts and feelings.

"Gary was easy to dislike from a parent's point of view. He drank heavily, drove too fast, and dropped out of school two years ago. But Tracy was infatuated with him, and my husband and I knew that if we forbade her to go out with him, she'd see him behind our backs.

"We felt powerless as we watched our daughter become more like Gary and his crowd every day. It was as if he'd cast an evil spell on our little girl, blinding her to intelligent and constructive decision making. We told ourselves that she was just going through a phase, but as the situation worsened, it became increasingly difficult to believe our own excuses. And after Tracy was sent home from school intoxicated a second time, we had to face reality."

◆ ◆ ◆ ◆

Teen alcohol abuse is often considered a family problem even if the teen in question is the only one who drinks. That's because sooner or later everyone in the family will be affected by the young person's behavior. The family often also helps to determine how the problem is handled as well as how soon outside help is sought.

Family Response to Teen Drinking

Sadly, many families respond to a young person's substance abuse in an unhealthy way. Just as the teenager often denies that a problem exists or that he or she is out of control, families often reject the notion that anything is genuinely wrong. Some cling to this belief despite the fact that their son or daughter either appears intoxicated or suffers from a hangover most mornings, or that substantial quantities of alcohol have vanished from their liquor stock.

When evidence to the contrary becomes overwhelming, they may admit that their child drinks while insisting that he or she only does so because of peer pressure or pressure from the people he or she dates. Embarrassed by the situation, the drinker's immediate family may erect a wall of secrecy around the issue. Everyone is continually warned not to let the grandparents or aunts and uncles know what's actually happening. Younger siblings may also be reminded not to tell their friends the "family's business." Yet this blanket denial merely reinforces the young substance abuser's rejection of reality and allows the young person to continue to believe that he or she can stop drinking whenever he or she wishes.

As the situation worsens, most families find it too difficult to go on ignoring what is really happening. In their desperation, some parents overzealously try to exert an extreme degree of control over the troubled teen's life. They impose excessive regulations on the drinker in a futile effort to reestablish their authority. This may entail driving their teenage son or daughter to and from school, forbidding the teen to see his or her friends, as well as checking to see that homework is done and there is no alcohol on the teen's breath.

Parents who formerly might have been too lax in setting appropriate limits often seem to suddenly turn into dictators. Although some teens temporarily respond to the new regimentation, the vast majority rebel within weeks, leaving the family more distraught than before.

Other families respond differently. Feeling they must do something to help, some parents, as well as siblings, assume the role of knight in shining armor. Often they'll spend quite a bit of money and energy bailing the teenage substance-abuser out of the alcohol-related trouble he or she has gotten into. This frequently includes providing him or her with extra money (since the teen can no longer keep a part-time job), hiring a lawyer to defend him or her if drinking has resulted in an arrest, and continually trying to persuade school authorities to give the teen "just one more chance."

While their intentions are admirable, in assuming responsibility for the teen drinkers' unacceptable actions, these parents deprive them of the opportunity to learn from their mistakes. The young people are shielded from a reality that may be much more difficult to cope with as time passes. Believing that somehow they'll always be rescued, young drinkers will usually continue their self-destructive use of alcohol.

Eventually the teen's family may become enraged at him or her for not changing in spite of their ongoing efforts to help. In their frustration, they've failed to realize that the teenage alcohol abuser is too out of control to fulfill either their hopes and dreams, or, his or her own.

Regardless of how a family initially responds to the problem, coping with a habitual teen drinker puts a drain on the entire household. Often other family members are seriously affected. The unrelenting tension can lead to divorce, alcohol abuse on the part of the parent(s), and numerous stress-related illnesses.

Frequently siblings of alcoholic teens experience sleep disturbances and eating disorders. Some start playground fights or become involved in substance abuse themselves. Many of these young people feel that after losing a brother or sister to alcohol, they also lost their parents once their father and mother became obsessed with their sibling's problem.

In many ways the family's interaction with the outside world is also altered. Everyone in the family unit may become increasingly isolated. Parents hesitate to invite other couples over to dinner or to play bridge because they feel too upset to be good company. Younger brothers and sisters frequently don't have their friends sleep over because they don't want to be embarrassed by the drinker's behavior or the loud arguments between their parents and sibling. The entire family may withdraw from various church, civic, and community functions as well.

Although at times family members may become exasperated with the alcohol abuser and want to give up on him, it's important for them not to completely turn away. If the young person is to remain part of the family unit, everyone involved will need to learn new, healthier ways of relating. The steps described below offer a good way to start.

Healthy Ways of Dealing with the Problem

Do Not Allow a Teen's Drinking Problem to Dominate the Family. While having a teenage drinker in the family cannot be ignored, it is important to keep the problem in proper perspective. Whenever possible, family events,

Students attending South Dakota's Improvisational Theater Training learn to cope with stress as well as how to teach these skills to others through dramatic skits. Such workshops can be useful to both young people who drink and their siblings.

vacations, and celebrations should continue as they have in the past. These necessary pressure-release valves are especially crucial for people attempting to grapple with what often proves to be a long-term problem.

The substance abuser's brothers and sisters must also remember that they have a right to continue participating in school, social, and other activities outside the home. While they can feel compassion for their sibling, they cannot afford to feel guilty for succeeding in areas where the drinker may have failed. Frequently, counseling is extremely beneficial in assisting siblings of teen alcohol abusers to deal with the wide spectrum of emotions they experience in response to their brother's or sister's drinking.

Acknowledge That the Substance Abuser Is Responsible for His Own Actions. The substance-abusing adolescent will not be helped by a family that continually makes excuses for his drinking. Seeing the problem is the first step toward solving it, and while it may be painful, it is crucial to own up to that reality. Teenagers do not drink because of the crowd they're in or because a boyfriend or girlfriend eggs her or him on to do so, but because the teens choose to.

Stop Enabling the Teen to Continue Abusing Alcohol. Many people find this step especially difficult, since they believe that they've been trying to help the teen alcohol abuser all along. At times, however, seemingly kind acts can actually have the reverse effect in the long run. What this step means is that an older brother or sister must have the strength to refuse when his addicted sibling pleads with him or her to buy alcohol. Both older and younger brothers and sisters need to stop covering up for the drinker when parents ask if they saw their sibling at school today or if he or she went out on Saturday night after the parents left the house. Everyone in the family must realize that they can best help the substance abuser if they allow the drinker to directly experience the consequences of the unacceptable behavior. Only then will the teen be motivated to accept outside help and gain the courage to change his or her life.

Improve Communication and Openness. Dark, hidden secrets can often be disastrous for both family relationships and the family's interaction with the outside world. Teen alcohol abuse is too overwhelming a problem to pretend it doesn't exist. It's important for everyone involved to have an opportunity to honestly discuss their feelings and reactions to the predicament and its impact on their lives. Since healthy families reflect concern for the well-being of all their members, it's important not to be critical of any one individual's response to what has occurred. Speaking frankly and remaining open about these issues also allows the family to benefit from outside educational and community support systems.

Even though he or she may initially resist, it is essential that the teen drinker eventually secure outside help. However, the family cannot hinge its happiness on the degree or speed of the substance abuser's recovery. Instead, family members must try to establish lasting bonds through shared feelings and compassion for one another.

Since a family that's dealt with substance abuse has generally undergone a significant degree of stress, it may help to engage in an enjoyable sport or activity that everyone can take part in. Some families functioned extremely well prior to the substance abuse problem and merely need to rediscover their old ways of relating and enjoying one another. However, other families with problem teen drinkers may be plagued by a host of other related problems. Such difficulties frequently include alcoholic parents, poor communication, and/or child abuse. These families may require special help.

Support for Siblings. If a teen substance abuser's sibling cannot find the companionship and support the sibling needs at home, turning to neighborhood resources may be helpful. In such instances, confiding in a trusted teacher, guidance counselor, the parent of a close friend, or a clergyman can prove extremely beneficial. Becoming active in church, a community center, or school-related activities can also dispel some of the loneliness and alienation the siblings can experience. An individual who has found a fulfilling source of support for his or her own needs can often respond more sympathetically to a teenage brother or sister with a drinking problem.

6

Getting Help

Sooner or later the teenage substance abuser will have to seek help. At times a process known as intervention can be instrumental in persuading the teen to enter a treatment program. In such instances, friends and family members together confront the teen drinker with indisputable evidence that a problem exists. Once the same information is confirmed by those around him or her, the young person frequently admits that assistance is needed. It's generally recommended that a qualified substance abuse counselor coordinate the process and that the family be aware of appropriate area youth-oriented treatment centers beforehand.

The types and sources of available assistance will depend to some degree on where an individual resides. Urban centers usually offer a greater variety of resources than isolated rural areas. But you can get a general idea of what's available in the vicinity by checking the yellow pages of your local telephone book under the following headings: alcoholic treatment centers; mental health centers; social services; and hospitals.

Student Assistance Programs (SAPs) are school sponsored referral programs for youths with substance abuse problems. Many students enter SAPs after being coaxed to do so by a friend or school faculty member. A SAP counselor speaks with and observes the student prior to suggesting a treatment center. A family doctor, school guidance counselor, or clergyman can also be useful referral sources. Two types of assistance are available to teenage drinkers: professional treatment or self-help alternatives. Both are discussed below.

Professional Treatment

This form of help involves such professionally trained health care workers as doctors, nurses, social workers and mental health counselors. Many of those working with adolescents in this field have a special understanding of the emotional and family problems commonly associated with alcohol abuse. Their services are usually provided through a hospital, mental health center, alcoholism treatment facility or private office setting.

Adolescents seeking professional help may become in-

Here at Clear Brook Lodge, a treatment center in Shickshinny, Pennsylvania, teens receive the treatment needed to help them overcome their drinking problems.

volved in either in-patient or out-patient treatment programs. In-patients check into a hospital or residential treatment center where most remain for one to two months, although some programs last even longer. Here the young patient lives in a controlled, drug-free environment while attending individual and group therapy sessions, as well as learning how he can avoid alcohol after going home. Once he's completed the program, he'll usually return to the facility at least once a week for ongoing therapy sessions to assist him in adapting to an alcohol-free life-style.

Long-term in-patient treatment frequently takes place in halfway houses. Young people live drug-free at this facility while, generally, leaving it during the day to work or attend school. Many such centers offer various forms of therapy and counseling, recreational activities, and relapse-prevention support within a family-like environment.

The alternative to in-patient care is out-patient treatment—the type of help received by most teen alcohol abusers. As an out-patient, the young person lives at home while either going to school or working and receiving the necessary treatment at a clinic or therapist's office. The teen will frequently attend individual and group therapy sessions as well as family therapy if it's determined that the family is a factor in the substance abuse.

This type of treatment generally continues for about six months, although some teens need to continue therapy for considerably longer periods.

After the teen has undergone a thorough physical examination, some treatment facilities may recommend that he be placed on an Antabuse maintenance program. Antabuse is a medication that causes nausea, vomiting, painful headaches, a drop in blood pressure, fuzzy vision, and breathing problems if alcohol is ingested while the drug is being taken. Although some young alcohol abusers feel they need Antabuse to stop drinking, the medication does not stop a person's urge to drink. It merely causes him to become violently ill if he does.

Self-Help Programs

For the teen drinker in need of assistance, these programs may serve as an inexpensive, readily available alternative to professional help. Perhaps the best known such program is Alcoholics Anonymous (A.A.). A.A. basically consists of a group of recovering alcoholics who hold group meetings to "share their experiences strength and hope with each other." Their goal is to "solve their common problem and help others recover from alcoholism." There are no age or educational restrictions for joining A.A.—the only requirement is "the desire to stop drinking."[1]

In addition to its general discussion meetings, A.A. offers individual attention or "sponsorship" to incoming members. However, the organization does not make medical or psychological diagnoses, provide nursing services, engage in education about alcohol, or offer religious services. A.A. has over 2 million members in the United States, Canada, and 134 other countries throughout the world.

Alcoholics Anonymous has constructed the following twelve-question quiz for teens who drink.

1. Do you drink because you have problems? To relax?

2. Do you drink when you get mad at other people, your friends or parents?

3. Do you prefer to drink alone, rather than with others?

4. Are your grades starting to slip? Are you goofing off on your job?

5. Did you ever try to stop drinking or drink less—and fail?

6. Have you begun to drink in the morning, before school or work?

7. Do you gulp your drinks?

8. Have you ever lost your memory due to your drinking?

9. Do you lie about your drinking?

10. Do you ever get into trouble when you're drinking?

11. Do you get drunk when you drink, even when you don't mean to?

12. Do you think it's cool to be able to hold your liquor?[2]

Any young person who can answer yes to even one of these questions should carefully examine how alcohol is affecting his or her life, and consider attending an A.A. meeting or seek another form of help.

Regardless of the type of treatment chosen, recovering from alcohol abuse is often a trying process. Most people find the first months of treatment and sobriety the hardest, for both the teenager and those who interact with him. Some recovering teens may claim that they've learned to control their drinking after just a few weeks of living sober. Yet these are usually the ones most likely to resume drinking. Other young people will admit that giving up alcohol is a struggle and, although they've remained sober, they may often seem anxious or depressed.

It's crucial that both the family and teenager not expect too much too soon. At times teens trying to abstain from alcohol have slipped back into their former self-destructive habits. While a relapse is always disappointing, the young person and his or her family should not give up. It's unrealistic to think that such a challenging and

James C., a native Alaskan teenager, returns from a wilderness ski trip. The wilderness experience is an important part of a unique substance abuse recovery program run by VOA (Volunteers of America) of Alaska.

complex problem can be resolved in a short period of time.

Teenagers who stay sober for at least ten months have an excellent chance of remaining sober. They will also reap other benefits as grades and relationships with those around them improve as well. Yet sober teens and their families may find that new problems soon arise to replace the old. After giving up alcohol, many teens realize that they now have to learn better ways of handling unpleasant feelings and situations, the very things that might have previously contributed to their drinking problem.

At these junctures, the young person should remain in close contact with the support networks he or she relied on throughout the early recovery period. Such challenges are usually easier if taken one day at a time. To enhance teens' chances for success, they and their families should attempt to establish a sense of mutual trust and respect.

Firmly based support networks are especially important once recovering teens are forced to deal with peer pressure to drink again. Some young people find it easier to refuse and stand by their decision than others. But those who find themselves in this predicament might try one of the following quick responses suggested by the

Department of Health and Human Services Office of Substance Abuse:

No thanks, I'd rather walk my pet python.

No way, I'm in a skateboarding contest today.

Uh-uh, I need all my wits about me to write my new rap song.

With you?

No thanks, I'm saving my bad breath for pepperoni pizza.

You must be kidding! If I'm going to ruin my body, I'd rather do it with a hot fudge sundae.

No, thank you. I need all my brain cells, so I'd rather have noodle soup.

No, thanks, my coach will leave me on the bench.

I'd rather not. I'm too special.

No thanks, I don't like the taste.

No thanks, I'm an all-American. I'll stick to milk.

Changing how we all think about alcohol is crucial since teen drinking has already destroyed too many young minds, bodies and lives. This reality is worsened by the fact that the younger people are when they begin to drink, the more likely it is that they'll be heavy drinkers later on. With at least 8 million young people using alcohol every week and almost half a million going on weekly binges, teenage drinking is a problem we cannot afford to ignore.

CONTRACT FOR LIFE

A Contract for Life
Between Parent and Teenager

Under this contract, we understand S.A.D.D. encourages all youth to adopt a no use policy and obey the laws of their state with regards to alcohol and illicit drugs.

Teenager   I agree to call you for advice and/or transportation at any hour from any place if I am ever faced with a situation where a driver has been drinking or using illicit drugs. I have discussed with you and fully understand your attitude toward any involvement with underage drinking or the use of illegal drugs.

_____
Signature

Parent   I agree to come and get you at any hour, any place, no questions asked and no argument at that time, or I will pay for a taxi to bring you home safely. I expect we would discuss this at a later time.
I agree to seek safe, sober transportation home if I am ever in a situation where I have had too much to drink or a friend who is driving me has had too much to drink.

_____
Signature

_____
Date

Distributed by S.A.D.D., "Students Against Driving Drunk"

Resource Directory

Federal Agencies Concerned with Alcohol Abuse

National Clearinghouse for Alcohol and Drug Information (NCADI)
P. O. Box 2345
Rockville, MD 20852
(301) 468-2600
NCADI is the chief National Information Center for citizen information on substance abuse issues.

Drug Alliance Office
ACTION
806 Connecticut Avenue, N.W.
Washington, DC 20525
(202) 634-9759

National Institute on Alcohol Abuse and Alcoholism (NIAAA)
Department of Health and Human Services
Room 14C-17
5600 Fishers Lane
Rockville, MD 20857
(301) 443-2954

National Institute on Drug Abuse (NIDA)
Department of Health and Human Services
Room 10-04
5600 Fishers Lane
Rockville, MD 20857
(301) 443-4577

National Institute of Mental Health (NIMH)
Department of Health and Human Services
Room 15C-05
5600 Fishers Lane
Rockville, MD 20857
(301) 443-4515

Office of Indian Education Program
Bureau of Indian Affairs (BIA)
Department of the Interior
Mail Codes 4659-MIB
1951 Constitution Avenue, N.W.
Washington, DC 20245
(202) 343-4071

Drug Enforcement Administration (DEA)
Demand Reduction Section
Department of Justice
Room 1203
1405 Eye Street, N.W.
Washington, DC 20537
(202) 786-4096

Safe Schools Program
National Institute of Justice
Room 805
633 Indiana Avenue, N.W.
Washington, DC 20531
(202) 272-6040

National School Safety Center
Office of Juvenile Justice and
Delinquency Prevention
Department of Justice
Suite 200
1680 Ventura Boulevard
Encino, CA 91436
(818) 377-6200

Drug and Alcohol Abuse
Prevention and Treatment
Office of Juvenile Justice and
Delinquency Prevention (OJJDP)
Department of Justice
Room 758
633 Indiana Avenue, N.W.
Washington, DC 20531
(202) 724-8491

Law-Related Education
Office of Juvenile Justice and
Delinquency Prevention (OJJDP)
Department of Justice
Suite 400
25 E Street, N.W.
Washington, DC 20001
(202) 662-9620

National Highway Traffic Safety
Administration (NHTSA)
Department of Transportation
Room 5232
400 Seventh Street, S.W.
Washington, DC 20590
(202) 366-9550

State Agencies Involved in Substance Abuse Prevention Education

Alabama

State Department of Education
Division of Student Instructional
Services
607-A State Office Building
Montgomery, AL 36130
(205) 261-5252

Governor's Drug Abuse
Policy Board
11 South Union Street
Montgomery, AL 36130
(205) 261-7126

Alabama Department of Mental
Health
P.O. Box 1710
Montgomery, AL 36193-5001
(205) 271-9246

Alaska

Alaska Department of Education
Drug-Free Schools Programs
P.O. Box F
Juneau, AK 99811-0500
(907) 465-2841

Alaska Department of Education
Rural & Native Education
Coordination
P.O. Box F
Juneau, AK 99811-0500
(907) 465-2800

Alaska Council on Prevention
7521 Old Seward Highway
Suite A
Anchorage, AK 99502
(907) 349-6602

Arizona

Arizona Department of Education
Chemical Abuse Prevention
1535 West Jefferson
Phoenix, AZ 85007
(602) 255-3457

Governor's Office
Office of Substance Abuse
Prevention
700 West Washington, 9th Floor
Phoenix, AZ 85007
(602) 255-3456

Arizona Department of Health Services
Office of Community Behavioral Health
700 West Washington, 9th Floor
Phoenix, AZ 85007
(602) 255-3456

Arkansas

Arkansas Department of Education
Special Project Program
No. 4 Capitol Mall, Room 405B
Little Rock, AR 72201
(501) 682-4474

Department of Human Services
Office of Substance Abuse Prevention
400 Donaghey Plaza North
P.O. Box 1437
Little Rock, AR 72203
(501) 682-6656

California

California Department of Alcohol and Drug Programs
111 Capitol Mall, Suite 450
Sacramento, CA 95814
(916) 445-0834

Colorado

Colorado Department of Health
Alcohol and Drug Abuse Division
4210 East 11th Avenue
Denver, CO 80220
(303) 331-8201

Connecticut

State Department of Education
Office of Substance Abuse, Health and Safety
165 Capitol Avenue, Room 369
P.O. Box 2219
Hartford, CT 06145

State Office of Policy & Management
Substance Abuse Mobilization
80 Washington Street
Hartford, CT 06106
(203) 566-7458/4414

Connecticut Alcohol and Drug Abuse Commission
999 Asylum Avenue
Hartford, CT 06105
(203) 566-7458/4414

Delaware

Office of the Governor
Alcohol and Drug Abuse Programs
Carvel State Office Building
820 North French Street
Wilmington, DE 19801
(302) 571-3210

Bureau of Alcoholism and Drug Abuse
1901 North DuPont Highway
New Castle, DE 19702
(302) 421-6101

District of Columbia

D.C. Department of Education
Drug-Free Schools Programs
1350 Pennsylvania Avenue, N.W.
Washington, DC 20004
(202) 727-0248

D.C. Commission of Public
Health
Office of Health Planning &
Development
425 Eye Street, N.W.
Room 3200
Washington, DC 20004
(202) 724-5641

Florida

Florida Department of Education
Educational Prevention Center
Knot Building
Tallahassee, FL 32399
(904) 488-6304

Department of Health and
Rehabilitation Service
Alcohol and Drug Abuse Program
1317 Winewood Boulevard
Tallahassee, FL 32399
(904) 488-0900

Georgia

Department of Human Resources
Alcohol and Drug Abuse Services
Room 319
878 Peachtree Street, N.E.
Atlanta, GA 30309
(404) 894-4786

Hawaii

Office of the Governor
Office of Children and Youth
426 Queen Street
Honolulu, HI 96813
(808) 548-7582/7583

Department of Health—Office of
Primary Prevention
1627 Kilauea Avenue, Room 421
Honolulu, HI 96816
(808) 735-5272

Idaho

Idaho Department of Education
Drug Education Office
Len B. Jordan Building
Boise, ID 83720
(208) 334-2165

Idaho Department of Health
& Welfare
Division of Family and Child
Services
450 West State Street
Boise, ID 83720
(208) 334-5700/5935

Illinois

Illinois State Board of Education
Program Support Office
100 North First Street
Springfield, IL 62777
(217) 782-3810

Department of Alcoholism &
Substance Abuse
222 South College
Springfield, IL 62706
(217) 785-9067

Indiana

State Department of Education
Drug-Free Schools Programs
State House, Room 229
Indianapolis, IN 46204-2798
(317) 269-9611

Indiana Department
of Mental Health
Division of Addiction Services
117 East Washington Street
Indianapolis, IN 46204-3647

Iowa

Iowa Department of Education
Substance Education Office
Grimes State Office Building
Des Moines, IA 50319
(515) 281-3021

Iowa Department of Public
Health
Office of the Director
Lucas State Office Building
Des Moines, IA 50319

Iowa Division of Substance Abuse
Colony Building, Suite 500
507 Tenth Street
Des Moines, IA 50319

Kansas

Office of the Governor
Drug and Alcohol Abuse
Administration
Capitol Building, 2nd Floor
Topeka, KS 66612
(913) 296-3011

State Rehabilitation Services
Alcohol and Drug Abuse Services
700 West 6th Street
Topeka, KS 66606
(913) 296-3925

Kentucky

State Department of Education
Substance Abuse Education
Branch
Capitol Plaza Tower, Room 1715
Frankfort, KY 40621
(502) 564-6720

Governor's Cabinet for
Human Resources
Division of Substance Abuse
275 East Main Street
Frankfort, KY 40621
(502) 564-2000

Department for Health Service
Substance Abuse Branch
275 East Main Street
Frankfort, KY 40601
(502) 564-2880

Louisiana

Louisiana Department of
Education
Bureau of Student Services
P.O. Box 94064
Baton Rouge, LA 70804-3480
(504) 342-3375

Department of Health &
Human Resources
Committee on Drug-Free Schools
and Communities
Office of Prevention & Recovery
from Alcohol and Drug Abuse
P.O. Box 52129
Baton Rouge, LA 70892
(504) 922-0722

Maine

Department of Education &
Cultural Service
Division of Alcohol and Drug
Education
Stevens School Complex
State House Station No. 57
Augusta, ME 04333
(207) 289-3896

Department of Human Services
Office of Alcoholism and Drug
Abuse Prevention
State House Station No. 11
Augusta, ME 04333
(207) 289-2781

Maryland

State Department of Education
Drug-Free Schools Programs
200 West Baltimore Street
Baltimore, MD 21201
(301) 333-2318

Department of Health &
Mental Hygiene
Alcohol and Drug Abuse
Prevention Unit
201 West Preston Street
Baltimore, MD 21201
(301) 225-6541

Massachusetts

Office of the Governor
Governor's Alliance Against Drugs
McCormack Building
Room 2131
One Ashburton Place
Boston, MA 02108
(617) 727-0786

Department of Public Health
Division of Alcohol and Drug
Rehabilitation
150 Tremont Street
Boston, MA 02111
(617) 727-8614

Michigan

Michigan State Board of Education
Department of Health Education
P.O. Box 30008
Lansing, MI 48909
(517) 373-2589

Office of Substance Abuse Service
3500 North Logan Street
P.O. Box 30035
Lansing, MI 48909
(517) 335-4837

Minnesota

Minnesota State Planning Agency
Anti-Drug Abuse Program
100 Capitol Square Building
550 Cedar Street
St. Paul, MN 55101
(612) 296-4854

Department of Human Service
Chemical Dependency Program
Division
Space Center
444 Lafayette Road
St. Paul, MN 55101
(612) 296-4574

Mississippi

State Department of Education
Drug-Free Schools Programs
550 High Street, P.O. Box 771
Jackson, MS 39205
(601) 359-3598

Department of Mental Health
Division of Alcohol and Drug
Abuse
1102 Robert E. Lee Building
Jackson, MS 39201
(601) 359-1297

Missouri

Missouri Department of
Mental Health
Division of Alcohol and Drug
Abuse
1915 Southridge Road
P.O. Box 687
Jefferson City, MO 65102
(314) 751-4942

Montana

Department of Institutions
Alcohol and Drug Abuse Division
1539 Eleventh Avenue
Helena, MT 59620
(406) 444-2878

Nebraska

Nebraska Department of Public
Institutions
Division of Alcoholism &
Drug Abuse
West Van Dorn & Folsom Streets
P.O. Box 94728
Lincoln, NE 68509-4728
(402) 479-5583

Nevada

Office of the Governor
Bureau of Alcohol and
Drug Abuse
505 East King Street, Room 500
Carson City, NV 89710
(702) 885-4790

New Hampshire

Department of Education
Alcohol and Drug Education
Office
State Office Park, South
101 Pleasant Street
Concord, NH 03301
(603) 271-2376

Department of Health &
Human Services
Office of Alcohol & Drug Abuse
Prevention
6 Hazen Drive
Concord, NH 03301-6525
(603) 271-4629

New Jersey

Department of Education
Drug and Alcohol Program
225 West State Street
Trenton, NJ 08625
(609) 984-1890

New Jersey Division of Alcoholism
Training, Prevention and
Education Unit
129 East Hanover Street
Trenton, NJ 08608
(609) 292-0729

New Jersey State Department of
Health
Division of Narcotic Drug Abuse
Control
CN-360, Room 100
Trenton, NJ 08625
(609) 292-4414

New Mexico

Liaison for Drug-Free Schools
Programs
Office of the Governor
Executive Legislative Building
Santa Fe, NM 87503
(505) 827-3000

Drug Abuse Bureau
P.O. Box 968
Santa Fe, NM 87504-0968
(505) 827-2587

New York

State Education Department
Bureau of Health & Drug
Education
Washington Avenue
Albany, NY 12234
(518) 474-1491

Executive Office of the Governor
Division of Substance Abuse
Services
Stuyvesant Plaza, Executive Park
Albany, NY 12203
(518) 457-2965

New York Division of Alcoholism
and Alcohol Abuse
194 Washington Avenue
Albany, NY 12210
(518) 457-5840

North Carolina

Department of Public Education
Division of Alcohol & Drug
Defense
210 North Dawson Street
Raleigh, NC 27603-1712
(919) 733-6612

Department of Human Resources
Division of Mental
Health/Mental
Retardation/Substance Abuse
Services
Albermarle Building, Suite 1122
325 North Salisbury Street
Raleigh, NC 27611
(919) 733-4506

North Dakota

Department of Public Instruction,
Office of Chemical Health
State Capitol
Bismarck, ND 38505
(701) 224-2769

Ohio

State Department of Education
Substance Abuse Section
65 South Front Street, No. 719
Columbus, OH 43266-0308

Drug-Free Schools Program
State Department of Health
246 North High Street
Columbus, OH 43266-0588

Ohio Department of
Mental Health
Bureau of Drug Abuse and
Alcoholism
170 North High Street, 3rd Floor
Columbus, OH 43266-0586
(614) 466-7893

Oklahoma

Drug Free Schools Programs
Office of the Governor
State Capitol
Oklahoma City, OK 73105
(405) 521-2345

Department of Mental Health,
Alcohol & Drug Abuse
4545 North Lincoln Boulevard,
Suite 100
Oklahoma City, OK 73152
(405) 521-0044

Oregon

Department of Human Resources
Office of Alcohol and Drug Abuse
Programs
301 Public Service Building
Salem, OR 97310
(503) 378-2677

Pennsylvania

Pennsylvania Department of
Health Office of Drug & Alcohol
Programs
N & W Building, Room 929
Harrisburg, PA 17108
(717) 783-8200

Rhode Island

State Department of Education
Office of Substance Abuse
Education
22 Hayes Street
Providence, RI 02908
(401) 277-2651

Department of Mental Health
Mental Retardation and Hospitals
Division of Substance Abuse
Substance Abuse Administration
Building
Cranston, RI 02920
(401) 464-2191

South Carolina

Department of Education
Substance Abuse Education Unit
1429 Senate Street
Columbia, SC 29201
(803) 734-8097

**South Carolina Commission on
Alcohol & Drug Abuse**
Division of Program Support
3700 Forest Drive
Columbia, SC 29204
(803) 734-9589

South Dakota

State Department of Health
Division of Alcohol & Drug Abuse
Joe Foss Building, Room 125
523 East Capitol Street
Pierre, SD 57501-3182
(605) 773-3123

Tennessee

Tennessee State Planning Office
Drug-Free Schools Programs
John Sevier Building, Room 307
500 Charlotte Avenue
Nashville, TN 37219-5082

Department of Mental Health
Division of Alcohol and Drug
Abuse
James K. Polk Building
505 Deaderick Street
Nashville, TN 37219
(615) 741-1921/4241

Texas

**Texas Commission on Alcohol
and Drug Abuse**
1705 Guadalupe Street
Austin, TX 78701-1214
(512) 463-5510

Utah

Utah State Office of Education
Drug-Free Schools Programs
250 East 500 South
Salt Lake City, UT 84111
(801) 533-6040

**Utah State Division of Alcoholism
& Drugs**
150 West North Temple, Room
350
P.O. Box 2500
Salt Lake City, UT 84102
(801) 533-6532

Vermont

Vermont Agency of Human Services
Office of Alcohol & Drug Abuse Services
103 South Main Street
Waterbury, VT 05676
(802) 241-2170

Vermont Agency of Human Services
Office of Administrative Services
103 South Main Street
Waterbury, VT 05676
(802) 241-2170

Virginia

Department of Mental
Health/Mental Retardation
Prevention, Information and Training Services
P.O. Box 1797
Richmond, VA 23214
(804) 786-1530

Washington

Department of Community Development
Drug-Free Schools Programs
9th and Columbia Building,
GH-51
Olympia, WA 98504
(206) 753-0307

State Bureau of Alcohol &
Substance Abuse
OB-44W
Olympia, WA 98504
(206) 753-3203

West Virginia

State Department of Education
Drug Education Programs
Capitol Complex, Building B-309
Charleston, WV 25305
(304) 348-9930

West Virginia Department of
Health
Division of Alcoholism & Drug Abuse
1800 Washington Street, East
Charleston, WV 25305
(304) 348-2276

Wisconsin

Department of Health and Social Services
Bureau of Community Programs
1 West Wilson Street
P.O. Box 7841
Madison, WI 53707
(608) 266-3719/267-8933

Wyoming

Department of Health & Social Services
Substance Abuse Programs
Hathaway Building, Room 362
Cheyenne, WY 82002
(307) 777-6493

Notes by Chapter

Chapter 1

1. Debra Rosenberg, "Bad Times at Hangover U," *Newsweek,* November 19, 1990, p. 81.

2. HHS News, "National High School Senior Survey," (Washington, D.C.: National Association of State Alcohol and Drug Abuse Directors, 1990), p. 4.

3. Morbidity and Mortality Weekly Report, "Results From the National Adolescent Student Health Survey," *Journal of the American Medical Association,* April 14, 1989, p. 2025.

4. D. F. Preuser and A. F. Williams, *Sales of Alcohol to Underage Purchasers in Three New York Counties and Washington D.C.* (Arlington, Va.: Insurance Institute For Highway Safety, 1991), p. 32.

5. Office of the Inspector General, *Youth and Alcohol: A National Survey* (Washington, D.C.: U.S. Department of Health and Human Services, 1991), p. 8.

6. L. N. Robins and T. R. Preysbeck, "Age of Onset of Drug Use as a Factor in Drug and Other Disorders," *In Etiology of Drug Abuse: Implications For Prevention.* NIDA Research Monographer 56. (Washington, D.C.: U.S. Department of Health and Human Services, 1985).

Chapter 2

1. David Elkind, "Teens and Alcohol," *Parents,* January 1991, p. 122.

2. S.A.D.D., "Club News . . . Capturing Student Interest," In *The News . . . Arizona S.A.D.D.* 7, Fall 1991, p. 5.

Chapter 3

1. ABC News, "20/20". Transcript # 1320 (May 7, 1993).

2. *Ibid.*

3. *Ibid.*

4. *Ibid.*

5. *Ibid.*

6. "Youth and Alcohol, A National Survey—Drinking Habits, Access, Attitudes and Knowledge. Do They Know What They Are Drinking? " Press Conference with the Inspector General. Statement: Surgeon General Antonia C. Novillo.

7. Mary Ellen Pinkham, *How to Stop the One You Love from Drinking* (New York: G. P. Putnam's Sons, 1986), p. 79.

8. Gary G. Forrest, *How to Cope with a Teenage Drinker: New Alternatives and Hope for Parents and Families* (New York: Atheneum, 1983), p. 20.

9. *Ibid.*

Chapter 6

1. Alcoholics Anonymous, *A.A. Fact File* (New York: A.A. World Services Inc., 1956), p. 1.

2. Alcoholics Anonymous, "A Message to Teenagers . . . How to Tell When Drinking Is Becoming a Problem" (New York: A.A. World Services Inc., 1988), p. 1.

Further Reading

Books:

Hyde, Margaret O. *Alcohol: Uses and Abuses*. Hillside, N.J.: Enslow Publishers, 1988.

Hyde, Margaret O. *Drug Wars*. New York: Walker, 1990.

Knox, Jean McBee. *Drinking, Driving and Drugs*. New York: Chelsea House, 1988.

Ryan, Elizabeth A. *Straight Talk About Drugs and Alcohol*. New York: Facts On File, 1989.

Silverstein, Herma. *Alcoholism*. New York: Franklin Watts, 1990.

Stepney, Roo. *Alcohol*. New York: Franklin Watts, 1987.

Articles:

Elkind, David. "Teens and Alcohol." *Parents Magazine*, (January 1991), p. 122.

Gusfield, Joseph R. "Risky Roads." *Society*, (March-April 1991), p. 10.

Hogan, Barbara. "Declaring War On Drugs: Teens Fight Back." *Teen Magazine*, (October 1990), p. 56.

Kent, Debra. "Sex While Intoxicated." *Seventeen*, (June 1991), p. 117.

LeBlanc, Adrian Nicole. "Drinking in America: Portrait Of a Teenage Drinker." *Seventeen*, (March 1990), p. 179.

Moore, Stacey. "Alcohol, the Teen Drug of Choice." *Redbook,* (March 1991), p. 10.

Porterfield, Marie Kay. "And the Loser Is . . . the Drinking Athlete." *Current Health,* (October 1990), p. 18.

Purdy, Cindy. "None for the Road." *Current Health,* (October 1990), p. 18.

Siler, Julia Flynn. "It Isn't Miller Time Yet, and This Bud's Not for You." *Business Week,* (June 24, 1991), p. 52.

Stanwood, Lee. "The Double Whammy of Alcohol and Drugs." *Current Health,* (October 1990), p. 26.

Trux, Suzy. "To Drink? Questions with Answers Only You Can Provide." *Current Health,* (October 1990), p. 12.

Index

A

adolescent rebellion, 53
advertising, as promoter of
    drinking, 45–49
alcohol
    accessibility of, 15–16
    as "gateway drug," 19
    history of use, in America,
        38–42
    physical dependence on, 18
    physiological effects of,
        16–18
    predisposition to, 51–52
    psychological attraction to,
        44–45
    risks of, 19–20
    See also drinking, teenage
alcohol-free social events, 34–36
Alcoholics Anonymous (A.A.),
    77–79
Antabuse maintenance program,
    77
antihistamines, and alcohol, 18
athletes, as sponsors of alcohol, 47

B

beer, alcohol content of, 20
binge drinkers, 43, 45
blood alcohol concentration
    (BAC), 27–31
bootleggers, 42

C

case histories
    beginnings of drinking
        problem, 7–11, 37

drinking and driving, 21–23,
    24, 25–27
family response to alcohol
    abuse, 62–63
warning signs of teenage
    drinking, 55–56
child abuse, 49–50
cirrhosis, 17
colleges, drinking at, 12–14, 42–45
Contract for Life Between Parent
    and Teenager, 31–33, *83*

D

delirium tremens (DT's), 18
denial, about drinking, 64–65
divorce, 49–50
drinking age laws, 14–15
drinking, teenage
    case histories. *See* case histories
    characteristics of, 37–38
    and driving, 21–36
    family response to, 62–72
    laws against, 14–15, 27–31
    magnitude of problem, 12–15
    medical emergencies from,
        11–12, 14
    reasons for, 15, 38–54
    treatment programs for, 73–82
    twelve-question quiz, 78–79
    volunteer programs against,
        31–36
    warning signs of, 55–61
driving, and drinking, 21–36
dry states, 41
DWI (driving while intoxicated),
    27–31

E

Eighteenth Amendment, 41–42
elementary school drinking, 14–15
emotional problems, and drinking,
    53–54

F

families
    isolation from, 57, 59–60, 67
    lifestyle of, and drinking, 49–51
    response to teenage alcohol
        abuse, 62–72
fetal alcohol syndrome, 17
fraternity drinking, 12, 14
friends, isolation from, 57, 59–60,
    67

H

halfway houses, 76
high blood pressure, 17
high school drinking, 15

I

in-patient treatment, 76
intervention, 73
isolation, from family and friends,
    57, 59–60, 67

J

Jell-O shots, 44
juvenile crime, and drinking,
    19–20

K

kegstanding, 44
Korsakoff's syndrome, 18

M

marijuana, and alcohol, 18
media, as promoters of drinking,
    45–49
Mothers Against Drunk Driving
    (M.A.D.D.), 33–34

N

National Commission Against
    Drunk Driving, 31

O

out-patient treatment, 76–77

P

parents, alcoholic, 49–51
    case history, 7–11
peer group pressure, and drinking,
    52–53, 81–82
pregnancy, and alcohol, 17
Prohibition Party, 41–42
psychological problems, and
    drinking, 53–54

R

recovery time, 79–81
"Red Ribbon of Hope," 34
resources, directory of, 85–96
responsibility, of parents vs.
    teenagers, for teenage drinking
    problems, 66–67, 69–70

S

school performance, and alcohol,
    19, 57–59
secrecy, about drinking, 64–65,
    70–71
self-help programs, 77–79
shotgunning, 44
siblings, 50, 66–67, 69, 70, 71–72
sleeping pills, and alcohol, 18
speakeasies, 42
sponsorship (A.A.), 78
sporting events, sponsored by
    breweries, 47
spouse abuse, 49–50
Spuds MacKenzie commercial,
    47–49

Student Assistance Programs
(SAPs), 74
Students Against Drunk Driving
(S.A.D.D.), 31, *32*, 36
suicide, 60

T
Teen Saferides, 33
temperance movement, in
America, 41
tranquilizers, and alcohol, 18
treatment programs
intervention, 73
professional, 74–77

recovery, time needed for,
79–81
self-help, 77–79
support networks, 81–82

U
ulcers, 17

W
whiskey, alcohol content of, 20
Whiskey Rebellion of 1794, 40
wine, alcohol content of, 20
Women's Christian Temperance
Union (WCTU), 41

About the Author

Elaine Landau has written over seventy-five books for children and young adults. She received her bachelor's degree from New York University and her master's degree in Library and Information Science from Pratt Institute.

She has worked as a newspaper reporter, an editor, and a youth services librarian. Ms. Landau says that many of her most rewarding hours have been spent researching and writing books for young people.